D1827526

Economists and the British Economy

Eighth Wincott Memorial Lecture
delivered at
The London School of Economics and Political Science
on Thursday 24 November, 1977

ALAN WALTERS

Professor of Political Economy,
Johns Hopkins University, Baltimore, Maryland

Published for
THE WINCOTT FOUNDATION
by
THE INSTITUTE OF ECONOMIC AFFAIRS
1978

First published in January 1978

by

THE INSTITUTE OF ECONOMIC AFFAIRS

for

THE WINCOTT FOUNDATION

Printed in Great Britain by

GORON PRO-PRINT LTD, LANCING, WEST SUSSEX

Set in Monotype Plantin

Contents

Preface

THE *Occasional Papers* were created primarily to make available essays and addresses of outstanding interest to audiences wider than those to which they were originally addressed.

Occasional Paper 54 reproduces Professor Alan A. Walters's Wincott Lecture, the 8th in the series, delivered to an audience at the London School of Economics on 24 November, 1977. The chair was taken, with his familiar grace and by now traditional classical allusions and Latin tags, by Mr Graham Hutton, Chairman of the Wincott Foundation.

The *Paper* is mainly a close dissection of 'the false theories – mostly but not entirely associated with Keynesian economics – [that] have been the bases of British economic policy for many years'. Here he deals mainly with the Phillips trade-off between unemployment and inflation, the relationship between consumption and income, and the investment function – the complex state of factors which determine private investment.

Perhaps as fundamental as these matters of technical/economic analysis is Professor Walters's question near the end of his lecture: 'Why do these false theories persist and why are they still accepted as the basis for the most far-reaching economic policies?' This is a recurring refrain that is implicit in many IEA *Papers*: IEA authors have demonstrated that the thinking behind post-war policies has often been false yet it is still taught in universities and schools, it is still discussed by newspapers as though it is true, and it is still believed by politicians and bureaucrats. The persistence of false economic thinking is a subject that will receive increasing attention in IEA *Papers* that will analyse the new development in economic theory: the economics of politics.

December 1977   ARTHUR SELDON

The Author

ALAN ARTHUR WALTERS has been Professor of Political Economy at the Johns Hopkins University, Baltimore, Maryland, since 1976. He was born in 1926 and educated at Alderman Newton's Secondary School, Leicester, and University College, Leicester (now the University of Leicester), graduating B.Sc.(Econ.) (London) with First Class Honours in 1951. From there he went to Nuffield College, Oxford, as a research student and thence to the University of Birmingham as a Lecturer in Econometrics in 1952. He was appointed Professor of Econometrics and Head of the Department of Econometrics and Social Statistics in 1961. Subsequently he was Sir Ernest Cassel Professor of Economics in the University of London (at the LSE), 1968-76.

Professor Walters was an Adviser in Operational Research to the Department of Health and Social Security, 1970-74, and a Member of the Roskill Commission on the Third London Airport, 1967-70. He has been a Consultant to the Governments of Israel, Singapore and Malaysia, and to the Economic Commission for Asia and the Far East. He has held visiting professorships at the University of Virginia (Autumn 1966), the Massachusetts Institute of Technology (1967), and Monash University, Melbourne (1970).

He has contributed widely to professional and learned journals, and his books (as author, contributor or editor) include: *Growth without Development* (1966); *The Economics of Road User Charges* (1968); *An Introduction to Econometrics* (1968, 2nd edn. 1970); and *The Economics of Ocean Freight Rates* (1969).

Professor Walters is a Trustee of the Wincott Foundation and a Member of the Advisory Council of the IEA, which has published his *Integration in Freight Transport* (Research Monograph 15, 1968), *Money in Boom and Slump* (Hobart Paper 44, 1969, 3rd edn. 1971), 'Land Speculator – Creator or Creature of Inflation', in *Government and the Land* (Readings 13, 1974), 'In Thrall to Creditors?', in *Crisis '75 . . .?* (Occasional Paper 43, 1975).

Economists and the British Economy
ALAN WALTERS

8th HAROLD WINCOTT MEMORIAL LECTURE

I

A REMINISCENCE

AT THE outset of this Lecture, I would like to record what a pleasure it was to have known Harold Wincott. In the late 1950s and early 1960s only a handful of British economists – for the most part associated with the IEA – began to swim against the mainstream of conventional wisdom of Cambridge, National Institute (NIESR), Treasury and Bank of England establishment. At first, the establishment ignored them – expecting, I suppose, that they would become weary once more and rejoin the mainstream. But the IEA went on its way. And the obloquy was poured in full measure: jejune, Neanderthal, antediluvian – ultimately becoming Selsdon man.[1]

Of course, all this robust criticism did have a point, for we were attempting to refloat many of the fundamental ideas of economics, which, it seemed to us, had long been regarded as sunk without trace.[2] We expected a long battle against the tide – and many of us were naïve enough to believe that ultimately accepted doctrine and even policy would change dramatically. But our wise and very experienced pilot, Harold Wincott, harboured no such illusions. He had a shrewd idea where the mainstream was leading, of the shoals and swamps of state control, and the inflationary spiral ahead. Reading again *The Business of Capitalism*,[3] one is struck by the fact that he not only had a firm grasp of fundamental principles but periodically produced penetrating insights into the behaviour of men and markets. I do not

---

[1] I thought that the ultimate accolade was awarded when one economist referred to the 'marketeers' as 'Seldon men'.

[2] The reader will notice that I have slipped into the first person plural – I believe I became involved with the IEA from 1959.

[3] Institute of Economic Affairs, 1968.

think that financial journalism had shown such wisdom since the golden days of Walter Bagehot.

'A sorry scramble'

In the last seven years, since the First Wincott Memorial Lecture was delivered by Professor Milton Friedman,[1] we have witnessed events which in Harold Wincott's days would have been regarded by the clerisy as unworkable, unthinkable, 'politically impossible', and inconsistent with social order. Britain has simultaneously suffered a massive inflation and rates of unemployment more than double what was thought unacceptable only a few years ago. The pound floats along with many other currencies. The grand 1963-65 crusade for growth has turned into a sorry scramble to prevent the decline and de-industrialisation of Britain. The search for scapegoats has introduced bitterness, divisiveness and recrimination. Now that the masses are under the delusion that they have the keys to the national treasury, even the most thoughtful observers are wondering whether democracy will survive.

II

LESSONS OF MACRO-ECONOMIC MANAGEMENT

MY MAIN purpose, however, is not to provide yet another review of this sorry tale. But the experience of Britain over the 1970s has furnished us with the most valuable tests of the conventional theories of macro-economics; and you will not be surprised to learn that the theory failed the tests. Thus, I shall reflect upon the curious process by which certain doctrines of macro-economics – and, one must add, particularly of Cambridge economics – manage to survive the most damning evidence that has been adduced to discredit them. It is surely worthy of note that notions of economics continue to be widely disseminated and accepted in spite of their inherent defects and of their lack of correspondence to reality of common observation. It would be interesting to explain *why* these false notions persist, but, although I shall speculate on the reasons, I am convinced I have not got an adequate or even a plausible explanation.

[1] *The Counter-Revolution in Monetary Theory*, Occasional Paper 33, IEA for the Wincott Foundation, 1970 (3rd Impression 1974).

[8]

These false theories – mostly but not entirely associated with Keynesian economics – have been the bases of British economic policy for many years. Thus it is natural that these concerns should be reflected in the themes chosen by the Wincott lecturers. Although I too cannot resist the temptation to comment with acerbity on the economic policy of successive British governments, such criticism must be at best incomplete and at worst misleading. Policy is determined by many considerations, only one of which is economics.

Yet it is still vitally important to examine critically the ideas, principles and theories of economics on which policy is based. And in British economic thinking, one can easily detect a recurring theme – that free markets will perform in an unsatisfactory way and give rise to unemployment and exploitation, externalities and social costs, inefficiency and excess. Massive government intervention is needed in order to ensure full employment, fair rewards, and the efficient allocation of resources.

On the other hand, the seven Wincott lecturers have pointed out that the free-market system did in practice exhibit impressive stability and efficiency. Government intervention – as well as the new monopolistic exploiters, the trade unions – had largely contributed to the mess of declining output and high unemployment as well as rapid inflation.[1]

In this, the Eighth Wincott Lecture, I shall review the plausibility of the main propositions on which the managers of the economy (Treasury and Bank) have leaned so heavily for so many years. You will all recall that one of those propositions, the 'Phillips curve', with its nice trade-off between unemployment and inflation, was convincingly discredited by experience in the late 1960s and early 1970s when both unemployment and inflation rose perversely together to new highs. Yet wage-rate rigidity or 'inflexibility' is still cherished as the heart of latter-day legitimate Keynesianism, and deserves at least a brief review.

---

[1] No doubt, it will be held that all the lecturers were adherents of the 'free market' and so one should not take their conclusions too seriously. Although this view may be tenable with respect to proposals for policy, it is completely irrelevant for judging the veracity of substantive propositions. Both theories and facts are amoral, and are independent of the motives of the proponent. We ought to judge propositions by their correspondence to the truth and not by the intentions of those who advance them.

The other two fundamental propositions of the theory of economic management – the consumption-income relationship and the investment function – remained more or less intact when these lectures began in 1970. I shall suggest to you that our experience during the mid-1970s has discredited the consumption (or savings) function as a basis for predicting economic events. This seems to be the most important lesson derived from the brute facts of the slump. A second lesson – perhaps somewhat less dramatic – is that we simply cannot account for that complex set of factors which determines the level of private investment. The behaviour of businessmen, just like the behaviour of households, was remarkably perverse during 1975-77 and no-one knows why.[1] That is the lesson of the 'recovery'.

Expectations – 'a fundamental misconception'
Many monetary economists conjecture that one of the main reasons for the difficulty in tracking the economy and the consequential inefficiency of the management of demand is a fundamental misconception about people's and businessmen's expectations and confidence. Recent reflections on this conundrum suggest that if anticipations of future events are formed in a sophisticated rather than a Pavlovian fashion, the prospects for accurately forecasting events and the management of demand are indeed bleak.

Finally, I shall review some of the fashionable explanations for the behaviour of the economy in the 1970s and I shall attempt an assessment of current thinking about the management of the economy. So it is convenient to begin in 1970 with the monetarist counter-revolution.

III

MONETARISM 1970

IN THE First Wincott Lecture in 1970, Milton Friedman discussed what he regarded as a notion free entirely from ideological commitment – the quantity theory of money. In 1970, he demon-

---

[1] Oddly enough, this will be a source of great satisfaction to many left-leaning Keynesians (such as Joan Robinson, who attributes investment to businessmen's 'animal spirits'). It provides a rationalisation for the control of investment by the state through the National Enterprise Board (NEB), etc.

strated that the quantity theory had not merely emerged from the closet in the United States (oddly enough, with the assistance of massive federal spending programmes financed largely by increased growth of the money supply!) where it had been preserved from extinction by a few eccentrics, but it had also developed a vigorous research programme that showed itself rather more capable than any other theory of explaining much of the history of boom and slump, inflation and deflation. The essence is simple: if the quantity of money is increased by a substantial amount, the 'price' of money (in terms of goods exchanged per unit of money) is likely eventually to fall. In other words, the general level of prices will rise.

It is, of course, merely an illustration, but a very famous one, of the laws of supply and demand. But it produced powerful and, to modern ears, surprising predictions. For example, if government spending were increased and the authorities acquired the money, not by 'creating' new cash, but by selling long-dated gilts to non-bank domestic residents, there would be no expansionary (or inflationary or reflationary) effect on the economy. Now anyone trained in the high Keynesian tradition would dismiss such notions as absurd; of course an expansion of government expenditure would have an effect.[1] Whether the increased spending was financed by selling gilts or creating money was a secondary concern and had very little or no consequence on the outcome. But, Friedman argued, in order to predict its effects, the nature of the financing of such expenditure mattered very much. Whether the spending was financed by creating money or by 'crowding out' private expenditure through the bond market determined whether the policy was or was not expansionary (inflationary, etc.).

Money does matter

To the clerisy of demand managers and their academic supporters, this was heresy. For many years – at least since the 1940s in Britain – it had been widely accepted that 'money did not matter', or at least that money mattered only for the purpose of preserving

---

[1] For example, if there were high unemployment, government spending would increase output and employment to higher levels both in the short and the long run. Government spending gave 'something for nothing'.

orderly financial markets. (Here I paraphrase Lord Kaldor.[1]) The monetarist counter-revolution showed not merely that 'money did too matter' but that it mattered a lot.

Yet I do not think that this particular conclusion was the main result of the counter-revolution. The primal point was that no model, whether monetary or Keynesian, could foretell accurately the performance of the economy over the next two years. The extensive empirical studies and the critical evaluation of existing 'models' of the world's economies showed how very *little* we knew about the determinants of the national economy. This was against the grain of contemporary wisdom. The belief was that, with Keynesian theory developed quantitatively, either formally in a model or through some more informal accounting framework, one could predict with a high degree of confidence where the economy was going over the next year or so. True, it was widely admitted that it was difficult to make good predictions about the behaviour of foreigners.[2] But with few disclaimers, it was commonly accepted that any body of Keynesian economists, suitably equipped and financed, could foretell, under the assumption of unchanged government taxes and spending, what would happen to the economy in the year or so ahead.

Confidence was no doubt nurtured by the unremarkable fact that all models tended to tell the same tale. Thus the government was advised on the adjustments in tax rates, government spending and controls on hire purchase so that any forecast shortcomings in the performance of the economy could be made good. Sailing analogies came readily to mind. Windblown Chancellors could find a receptive and appreciative audience when they talked of 'a touch on the tiller', 'leaning against the breeze', 'steady as she goes', and so on. The steering instruments were always taxes, government spending, hire purchase controls, bank rate, but never the money supply.[3]

---

[1] 'The New Monetarism', *Lloyds Bank Review*, July 1970.

[2] Oddly enough, however, the New Cambridge School claimed that it was much easier to forecast the balance of payments than other elements. The New Cambridge economists have rather a Lady Bracknell view of the foreign balance; it is simply the residual after the government has determined its financial deficit.

[3] On returning from the United States in 1959 just after publication of the Radcliffe Report, I was surprised to learn that there was no statistical series on the money supply in the United Kingdom. But since the vast body of

[*Contd. on page 13*]

No reliable controls in short run

A common but understandable misinterpretation of the teaching of the monetarist counter-revolution is that the quantity of money should be used to control the economy – rather than taxes and government spending. This is almost the opposite of the intent. The primal conclusion is that *no* instruments of policy, whether money or taxes or spending, have well-defined and precise, predictable consequences in the short run, that is to say, over a period of up to two years. True, Friedman and many others (such as the economists at the Federal Reserve Bank of St. Louis) have pointed out that the monetary model performs rather better than the Keynesian paradigm for a two-year horizon; but both predict very poorly.

In part, this performance is poor because extraneous, unforeseen and often unforeseeable events play a large role in determining economic conditions: famine and flood, trade unions and terrorists, political manoeuvring and foreign conspiracies – all influence economic conditions. There *is* a large element of chance. However, such chance elements may be tractable or at least tolerable if one could rely on certain constants of economic theory. Alas, our experience over the 1970s has shown that those 'constants' upon which the massive edifice of macro-economics is built are given to dis-obliging shifts which occur unfortunately when the forecaster most needs them to stand still.

IV

Consumption and Savings in the 1970s

One quite remarkable example of this occurred in the slump of 1974-76. Keynesian theory hinges on the stability of the consumption function – that is to say, on a stable and predictable relationship between the disposable income of persons and their spending on real goods and services. For many years this relation-

[Contd. from page 12]

    evidence to Radcliffe had asserted that the money supply was of little or no importance, it was understandable that no-one thought it worthwhile to measure it. I believe that the first comprehensive series on the stock of money was produced at the University of Birmingham in 1960-63.

ship has exhibited a long-run stability: in the United States, people spent about 90 per cent of their income; in Britain, the rate was somewhat higher at 92 per cent. In the short run, there was some variation about this value; but the variation was reliable and therefore predictable. Friedman himself contributed to this body of knowledge with what is, I believe, still his finest work, by demonstrating that a very wide variety of evidence was consistent with this so-called 'permanent income theory of consumption'.[1] It seemed that, if there were a dependable constant in economics, this was it.

Economic theory confounded, 1974-75

Yet, during 1974-75 in Britain, everything seemed to go wrong. Consumer spending fell far more than anyone had predicted – to less than 87 per cent of income. And the ratio of personal savings to disposable income rose from its normal 8 per cent to over 12 per cent. Nor was this confined to Britain; virtually all Western countries (and Japan) experienced the same surge in savings in the slump.[2] And savings ratios have remained far higher than normal and show no sure signs of falling to what was regarded as their historically normal levels.

No economist correctly predicted such events. Indeed, as the Americans would say, no-one was even in the 'right ballpark'; so it is worth reflecting at length on this remarkable story of savings. It was the first important test of the stability of saving and consumption functions since the Second World War. The changes in incomes in 1974-76 were very large indeed and so provided a powerful test of the theory. Now the accepted principles of the consumption function allowed that there would be deviations from these constant overall marginal rates of saving. Cambridge economists (Lord Kaldor and Joan Robinson in particular) had long argued that the savings rate of workers was much lower than that of rentiers. (So important was this principle to them that the whole edifice of the Cambridge theory of the distribution of income was built upon it.[3]) Thus, a redistribution of income

---

[1] *A Theory of the Consumption Function,* Princeton University Press, Princeton, N.J., 1957.

[2] For Japan, for example, the savings ratio in 1960-73 was around 19 per cent; for 1974-76 it was more than 25 per cent—an increase of over 30 per cent.

[3] The proportion of income going to rentiers had to be just high enough to ensure that savings equalled the predetermined level of investment.

from workers to capitalists *would* give rise to a higher overall savings rate. In 1974-76, however, the massive redistribution was indeed unprecedented – but in *the opposite direction, from the rentiers to workers*. The Cambridge theory was not just wrong; it was perverse – *savings went up instead of down.*[1]

Lest anyone should harbour an inkling of a suspicion that I have a bias against Cambridge, let me immediately admit that the versions of the consumption function proposed by monetarists, such as the permanent income hypothesis of Friedman, gave rise to predictions which were belied by events. As real incomes fall temporarily below the long-term trend, as they did in the slump of 1974-76, Friedman's theory forecasts that real consumption would fall only slightly and so the savings ratio would fall quite steeply. *Perversely, it rose.*

And I must confess *mea culpa.* Readers of the 1974 *Sebag Gilt-edged Review* will see that I too thought that savings would fall. The combination of a persistent negative real rate of return, a government openly hostile to the saver and determined to make the pips squeak, and the likelihood of expropriation – all seemed to point to transfer from private provision for the future to more reliance on government handouts. I too was quite wrong.

Popperian falsification principle ignored

To the informed non-economist, the experience of the 1970s would be regarded as sufficient to discredit this bed-rock of Keynesian economics. If the Karl Popper principle of falsification is applied in the social sciences, this surely is a case to which it is germane. Yet we may observe that this refutation of the consumption function has made little impact. Everywhere, teachers and textbooks continue to assert the fundamental stability of the relationship. The tendency is to regard the 1970s as an anomaly, or perhaps as a once-and-for-all change to higher savings. Advisers make *ad hoc* adjustments to their forecasts.

In any case, there were many *ex post facto* rationalisations of this extraordinary event. It was argued, for example, that the expropriated households were trying to restore the value of their assets, and that the slump had enormously increased the demand for precautionary liquid assets. Alternatively, it was suggested

---

[1] From April 1974 to April 1975, real wages increased by 12·7 per cent.

[15]

that the redistribution of income and wealth from middle class to miners and other wage earners gave rise to high transitory savings (but these would presumably disappear as the miners bought their Volvos). Any or all of these may be true – but excuses of hindsight do not eradicate the errors of prediction.

V

The Discrediting of 'New Cambridge'

The high savings of 1974-75 discredited the theory of the New Cambridge School just when it was being weaned from infancy in the pages of *The Times* to its presentation to the Public Expenditure Committee of the House of Commons in the summer of 1974. The New Cambridge Theory regarded the financial surplus of the private sector as being approximately constant at about £800 million per annum. Then, as a matter of accounting, it follows that a financial deficit of the public sector would be reflected in an overseas financial deficit of the same amount, less the £800 million which the private sector would reliably contribute year in, year out. (Hence, the ease with which the New Cambridge School forecast the 1973-74 financial deficit on the balance of payments.)

'Unforeseen and unprecedented' rise in savings

In 1974-75, however, the rise in the savings rate of the personal sector, together with the rapid accumulation of liquid assets of the corporate sector, saw the financial surplus of the private sector leap to over £6,000 million. This was an *eightfold* increase in the surplus – quite unforeseen and unprecedented. Thus the financial deficit of the public sector was in large part financed by the private sector buying financial assets issued by the public sector – and the financial deficit overseas shrank remarkably.

It is difficult not to feel a touch of sympathy for New Cambridge. It was widely believed – and by many competing forecasters perhaps widely feared – that they had discovered the keys to the Keynesian kingdom. It is rare that a theory is so quickly discredited by contemporary history. We might also suppose that, after this experience, it would no longer be necessary to preach the virtues of humility to those economists who were prominent in New Cambridge in promoting the virtues of 'steering the economy'. But not so! Policies of protection, import quotas, expansionary government spending, etc., are still being assiduously propagated.

What happened to investment?

The savings-income relationship is only one of the props of conventional macro-economics. Another is investment. If the lesson of slump was to show that we could not predict savings, then the discovery of the recovery is that we cannot forecast domestic fixed investment. In virtually every Western country, governments have been told that there would be a rapid increase in investment in 1976-77. But there has been no confident surge, only a tremulous trickle. As with savings, there has been a rash of *ex post facto* explanations for the shortfall. But even the rationalisation that appeals to most people, the loss of confidence (in profitability) by the business community, merely substitutes one unknown for another; it simply provides another label for our ignorance. All 'explanations' are empty, untested propositions.

The investment experience is not such a dramatic reversal for conventional macro-economics as the story of savings. Private fixed investment has not actually fallen during the 1976-77 recovery – it has shown some increase, but far, far less than anyone had anticipated.[1] Yet it is accepted that, for appropriate macro-demand management, it is crucially important to be able to forecast investment by the private sector. It is one of the key elements of aggregate autonomous expenditure – the main determinant, *via* the multiplier, of the level of income and employment. If we cannot accurately forecast investment then no confidence can be placed in the prediction of income and employment.

Rigidities – the new vintage

Thus, I conclude that not only the stability of the consumption function but also the tractability of the investment relationship are now discredited. I am tempted to continue to what many

---

[1] For example, the CBI survey of investment intentions showed first a 15 per cent increase in 1977 on (October) 1976. But now (October 1977) there is a a doubt whether there will be *any* increase.

consider to be the third prop of Keynesian economics – the downward rigidity of money wages.[1] Of course, with money wage-rates rising by anything between 10 and 35 per cent per annum over the 1970s, whatever may have been the use of such a postulate during the slump of 1929-33, one may be forgiven for regarding any such downwards rigidity as now rather otiose. But some sort of inflexibility is needed by modern macro-economists, and two varieties are discernible.

First, it is said that the *rate of growth of money wages* cannot be deflected downward from its previous path; there is a floor to the rate of inflation of money wages.[2]

Secondly, that most distinguished Nobel Laureate, Sir John Hicks, has argued that there is now a rigidity in the level of *real* wages.[3] Fortunately there is no problem of choosing between them; both propositions have been convincingly discredited by events. The rate of growth of money wages has fallen remarkably over the years 1975-77, and the level of real wages, after showing a record rise of 12 per cent (April 1974 to April 1975), has fallen – again at record rates – for two years. What remains, therefore, of this proposition of inflexibility I leave you to judge.

---

[1] The failure of wage rates to adjust and clear the markets is, according to Joan Robinson, the true Keynesian theory; those who argue that the liquidity preference postulate is the essential element of Keynesianism are, according to her taxonomy, 'bastard Keynesians'. Most Americans are bastards, but not all bastards are American!

[2] I must confess that I can find no precise statement of what distinguished macro-economists mean by inflexibility or downward rigidity of money wages and indeed prices. Much is ascribed to these concepts by, for example:
'. . . the Monetarists were relatively optimistic about the possibility of deflecting money wages downward *from their previous path*, . . .' – Miller (Italics added.)
'. . . there have been major shifts in the United Kingdom in *relative* prices since the war [World War II], but one would be hard put to substantiate that there have been widespread falls in *absolute* prices . . .' – Ball and Burns (Italics in original.)
M. H. Miller, 'Can a Rise in Import Prices be Inflationary and Deflationary?', *American Economic Review*, September 1976, pp. 501-519;
R. J. Ball and T. Burns, 'The Inflationary Mechanism in the United Kingdom Economy', *American Economic Review*, September 1976, pp. 467-484.

[3] 'What is Wrong with Monetarism', *Lloyds Bank Review*, No. 118, October 1975, pp. 1-13. Sir John used the term 'real wage resistance' to describe this downward rigidity.

VI

The Counter-revolution in Expectations

By this point, you will have realised that I have considerable sympathy with what I take to be the real thrust of the counter-revolution – that is to say, that we know little about the forces that determine detailed economic conditions, such as prices and employment, exports and imports, output and productivity, savings and investment. True, the monetarists' results showed that the rate of inflation was ultimately determined by the excess of the rate of growth of the money stock over the rate of growth of real national income. True, also, the variations in the growth of the money supply had some transitory effects on employment and output; but all were highly uncertain both in timing and in magnitude. A government could do no good and, on the average, would probably inflict much harm by trying to fine-tune the economy – and this holds true whatever the instrument used, whether monetary or Keynesian. I have great sympathy for this view. Thus the best that can be done is to pursue a moderate and stable growth rate of the money stock – Friedman's famous rule.

The problem of expectations

Since Friedman's lecture in 1970 there has been much additional reflection on the fundamental dilemma of discretionary policy (as distinct from a simple rule), much of which has centred on the problem of expectations.[1] The treatment of expectations is one of the most uncomfortable aspects of economics. For many years economists normally treated both business men and housewives as though they were idiots who simply extrapolate their past experience into the future. Current events, however momentous, were supposed not to affect their views of the future. Now this was a wild and wilful travesty, as any housewife or business man knows. People *do* take account of current events in forming and reforming their anticipations of the future. I am persuaded not only that business men and housewives *are knowledgeable* about predicting the future; I am prepared to believe that they are as successful, or unsuccessful, as the economists.

---

[1] For example, Milton Friedman, *Unemployment versus Inflation?*, Occasional Paper 44, with a British Commentary by David Laidler, IEA, 1975 (3rd Impression 1977).

'A game of attrition'

Suppose, therefore, that people expect what the economic theory predicts. (In my writings, I have called these *consistent* expectations, but they are usually known by the more presumptive title of *rational expectations*.[1]) But if people are as clever as economists, and if government policy operates according to economic models, then people will quite nicely offset the government's behaviour. For example, if people know that an increase in the rate of growth of the money supply will increase the rate of inflation, then they will adjust their behaviour (such as switch to gold or commodities) – and then the government must take this reaction into account in formulating their policies – but people will know this, and so it goes on. The normal concept of discretionary fiscal or monetary policy has now disappeared; it is a game – and a very serious game – of attrition.[2]

Examples of these games appear daily in the financial press. (And, in his perceptive way, Harold Wincott observed them many years ago.) In the textbooks, an increase in the rate of growth of the money supply is still said to reduce interest rates. In his Wincott Lecture, Friedman himself said that an increased rate of money growth will tend at first to reduce interest rates.[3] But now we know it does nothing of the kind; on the contrary, it *raises* them. Any market operator seeing an extraordinary increase in the money supply will know that the authorities are likely to tighten credit in the near future; consequently he will sell gilts and bonds in anticipation of the authorities' reaction. Then interest rates will rise.[4] Then the authorities are induced to play a double – bluff – but, of course, the clever market operators are quickly on to that.

[1] A. A. Walters, 'Consistent Expectations, Distributed Lags and the Quantity Theory', *Economic Journal*, June 1971.

[2] Incidentally, it is often alleged that the authorities really *know* the system they are managing – after all, they have unrivalled access to data and resources. So they would always win. I doubt this. The private operators have much incentive to win, whereas the bureaucrats have different aims.

[3] *The Counter-Revolution in Monetary Theory, op. cit.,* p. 25.

[4] But, you may object, this is merely the impact effect – surely, after a while' the additional money would flood into financial markets and so drive interest rates down. But not so. It would increase expectations of inflation and this would induce people to invest in assets denominated in real rather than monetary terms. Thus the demand for financial assets would diminish, depressing their price and increasing the yields.

A return to rules

One of the generalisations on which, I suspect, there may be virtual unanimity is that the private operator is much more adept at the market game and more fleet of foot than the bumbling bureaucrat. The authorities must expect to find their policy anticipated, frustrated, and offset. Games of this kind may be condemned as destructive. Certainly, at a very minimum they result in a diversion of activity into destructive stratagems – City trying to outguess the authorities and the Bank and Treasury duly bluffing and counter-bluffing.

One way in which the game-playing can be avoided is by the authorities eschewing discretionary policy and pursuing a fixed rule – by increasing the money supply at a fixed percentage rate or by aiming at a suitably 'standardised' public sector financial deficit.[1] The authorities should follow rules (of law?) rather than attempt to manage the system. Then government's behaviour would become virtually entirely predictable and the power of politicians to reward one group at the expense of another (to buy votes with other people's money) would be reduced. This reflects a great and abiding principle of constitutional government which was so eloquently and persuasively put by Professor F. A. Hayek in the Fourth Wincott Lecture.[2]

The effects of the counter-revolution

But, if I am correct in reinterpreting Friedman's 1970 message as really a return to rules, whatever became of his counter-revolution? Was it really successful in capturing the minds of the mandarins? Economic policy in Britain provides the most dramatic evidence of its immediate failure to convince anyone in the corridors of power. The rise in unemployment in the years 1970 and 1971 apparently induced the Conservative Government to embark on a massive expansion of deficit spending. Notwithstanding the mountain of evidence that Friedman and others had adduced to show that money does matter, from September 1971 the government began to expand the money

---

[1] Of course, not all games will be rendered otiose by the fixed rules; but they will be much smaller and well-contained in a narrow framework.

[2] *Economic Freedom and Representative Government*, Occasional Paper 39, IEA for the Wincott Foundation, 1973 (2nd Impression 1976).

supply (M_3) at a rate which, for two years, never fell below 20 per cent per annum and often hovered at 30 per cent. Could one find a more convincing case that the counter-revolution had been repulsed – indeed, was held in contempt – by the clerisy of Britain?[1]

In 1970-73, this disdain was reflected in the various macro-econometric models – those of the London Business School, the NIESR, and, so far as one can see through the veil of secrecy, of the Treasury. All these models have their focus on the short-term conditions of the economy. Their basic objective is to give guidance on fiscal policy – to provide advice for the Chancellor in the frequent budgets (and other adjustments to the 'tiller'). Thus, the models purport to show where the economy would be in the months ahead without any change in tax rates or government spending, etc. Then, in order to restore full employment and promote economic growth, the amount of money to be injected into the system is calculated, and suitable adjustments are suggested for the Chancellor's budget.

The Treasury model, even as late as 1974, did not contain the money supply at all. And in the London Business School model (1972), the money supply entered only into the determination of the cost of capital. Clearly the counter-revolution had received short shrift in the macro-econometric models. Moreover, these models followed Keynesian (perhaps one should say Kahn-Kaldor-Harrodian) methodology in another, perhaps more fundamental, sense: the price level was regarded as largely given.[2] For many years the current rate of inflation was thought to be determined by the current rate of unemployment – the higher the rate of unemployment, the lower the rate of inflation. But the experience of simultaneous high unemployment and inflation

---

[1] A witty and clever response by a most distinguished member of the clerisy to the mounting evidence of monetarism was Lord Kaldor's lecture, 'The New Monetarism', at University College, London, on 12 March, 1970, published in *Lloyds Bank Review*, July 1970. I believe that this speech was most influential in confirming the clerisy in the comforting conclusion that monetarists were cranks. The important persons could get on with the really important business of running the economy.

[2] Indeed, in this sense the modellers were perfectly consistent; the effects of the money supply on prices are in the longer term (i.e., over two to five years), while their concern was normally more in the shorter term than in the longer run.

has left the Phillips curve friendless.[1] In one sense, this result has had an important consequence. If one cannot contain an inflation by increasing unemployment, then there is no excuse for 'tolerating' a large volume of unemployment.

VII

COST-PUSH AND EXPANSIONISM

BUT, IN any case, the fall of Phillips left the rate of inflation just hanging there. It remained to be explained. And it is clear that most of the clerisy regarded (and, I believe, still regard) the rate of inflation as being determined by cost-push – in particular, by the monopolistic behaviour of trade unions and also by the largely independent behaviour of foreigners such as sheiks who demand high prices for their oil.

This 'cost-push' explanation of price change, particularly that due to monopolistic unions, comes in many forms. Some of the most sophisticated, such as that of Mr Peter Jay in the Sixth Wincott Lecture,[2] argue that the unions raise wages, cause unemployment and so induce the government to expand the money supply, etc., in order to reduce unemployment to levels consistent with electoral requirements. And this generates accelerating inflation. Thus the cost 'push' is through the *political* process rather than direct. And I would agree that this political cost-push was undoubtedly responsible for much of the inflation in Britain in the 1960s and early 1970s.

Simplistic 'cost-push' versions

But I suspect that the vast majority of economists, politicians and informed people hold somewhat more simplistic versions of cost-push; they regard monetary conditions as either self-accommodating or largely outside the control of the authorities. Yet the evidence of the past few years (end-1973 to November 1977) has

---

[1] There is no evidence of the modellers embracing the more sophisticated 'expectations-augmented' Phillips curve of Professors Friedman and E. S. Phelps.

[2] *A General Hypothesis of Employment, Inflation and Politics*, Occasional Paper 46, IEA for the Wincott Foundation, 1976 (2nd Impression 1977).

shown that, as in 1968-69, where there is a will there is a way. Monetary expansion has been contained. And in November 1977, much against the passionate advocacy of its erstwhile advisers, the Government allowed sterling to appreciate rather than loosen the monetary strings.[1] The crude cost-push theory regards such monetary discipline as largely irrelevant.

Another remarkable characteristic of economic thinking of the 1970-73 period was that it was still asserted that under conditions of quite modest levels of unemployment an increase of public expenditure would give rise to an increase in real output. There was little 'crowding out' and no large expansion of imports (and reduction of exports). Thus by expanding public spending the economy got something for nothing. Employment and output would grow with little or no effect on the rate of inflation.[2]

Barber's boom and rationalisation

Of course, with mature reflection on these 'something for nothing' convictions we should not be astonished by the reaction of the Conservative Government.[3] The same protestations of outrage that we hear today with more than one and a half million unemployed were even louder in 1971 with less than one million on the dole. Received and respected opinion, buttressed by the predictions of the models, showed that expansionary public spending and money supply from September 1971 onwards would not bring about significant increases in inflation. On the contrary, they would merely mop up the pool of unemployed. The siren's song of 'something for nothing' was too strong to resist. And the

[1] See the letter dated 29 October by Lord Kaldor in *The Times*, 1 November, 1977. Lord Kaldor would allow the appreciation of sterling only if there were a general *ad valorem* duty of 20 per cent on all manufactures and an additional 10 per cent on 'sensitive items'. This programme would 'stop inflation', create an investment boom and recreate full employment. He then goes on to argue that such a policy would also generate a high growth rate.

[2] I have discussed the characteristics of macro-economic models in 'Macro-economic Models and Policy in Britain', in Michael Intrilligator (ed.), *Frontiers of Econometrics*, North Holland, 1977. Since I wrote that article in 1975, the models have been through many metamorphoses. In particular, the London Business School (LBS) model has incorporated many lessons from experience in the 1970s. And in the discussion of policy implications by Messrs T. Burns and A. Budd there has been a considerable movement towards the monetarist approach.

[3] I must confess, however, that at the time, the Heath-Barber policy *did* greatly surprise me.

arguments of monetarism sounded negative, anti-social and even anti-Conservative: conventional expansionism prevailed.

You all know what happened in 1973-75. The inflation which was predicted by monetarists duly occurred on schedule. Prices and incomes controls were duly introduced. The balance-of-payments deficit turned out to be far worse than even monetarists had predicted – and this result was partly due to the increased price of imports.

How the discredited conventional wisdom was restored

One would have thought that such a massive discrediting of the conventional wisdom would have had a considerable effect on the profession and the Treasury. But such investment of time and effort had gone into the development of these demand management ideas that they were not to be lightly discarded. Nor should they be. Even the most successful and progressive theories have small anomalies and odd discrepancies. One swallow, however gigantic, does not make a summer. Indeed, attempts to explain away the 1974 inflation have normally taken two courses.

First, it is argued that the increase in the rate of inflation was entirely due to the extraordinary rise in the price of imports – something over which Britain is said to have no control.[1] Nor can one expect to predict such extraordinary events as the oil cartel, etc.

It is easy to show, however, that Britain's extraordinary inflation got under way with a current overseas deficit that more than offset the higher price of imports.[2] In 1973-74, we were *exporting* inflation, not importing it. Furthermore, it is clear that other countries such as Germany and Japan, suffered similar rises in world prices of their imports yet their inflation rates were about one-quarter and one-third of those in Britain. The point is, that although the import price rise entailed a loss of real income, the governments of the day pursued expansionary policies and paid for them with overseas borrowings. Reality was postponed for a year or two. No doubt, the aims were noble – to keep down the

---

[1] Of course, we do. The government has willingly entered into various restrictive agreements to maintain the price of many of Britain's imports. Coffee, wheat, sugar, shoes and shirts are examples.

[2] A. A. Walters 'Importing and Exporting Inflation', *International Currency Review,* November-December 1973. pp. 7-10.

level of unemployment, to maintain incomes and to provide the world with an expanding British demand to offset the restricted demand of other countries – and were not calculated to win elections. But the results were sad.

The slump and the slowing of inflation

Since the world price of imports did not continue its rise relative to the price of Britain's exports in 1975-76, it was hardly possible to ascribe the continuing inflation to import prices. So the *second* and most important rationalisation for inflation was brought into play – the union-cost-push. And since the unions are an independent force, the only way to control them is by a body of legislation (or administrative extra-legal controls) which somehow limits their ability to generate inflation. Great ingenuity has been lavished on this problem – and, in the second Wincott Lecture, Professor James Meade[1] provided what seems to me to be the best proposal so far that is consistent with the widest possible measure of freedom. I believe that most British economists accept that some sort of wage control is now a necessary, though not a sufficient, condition for the control of inflation. Indeed the experience of the 1970s – particularly the massive wage explosion in 1974-75 – lends plausibility to the view that wage control is the *only* way.[2]

The majority of men of affairs regard the £6 a week pay policy which was imposed in mid-1975, after the fiasco of the 'social contract', as an important or perhaps the main cause of the slowing-down of inflation from 1975.[3] Yet the sharp and prolonged slump of 1974-76 and the consequent slowing-down in the rate of inflation from 1975 was uncompromisingly predicted by monetar-

---

[1] *Wages and Prices in a Mixed Economy*, Occasional Paper 35, IEA for the Wincott Foundation, 1971.

[2] So ubiquitous is this view that sterling waxes and wanes according to the state of the unions. It would be painful to record yet again the massive evidence that has been accumulated on the inefficacy of wage and price controls. The fact that they are now widely regarded as the lynch pin, the *sine qua non*, of received opinion on macro-economic policy gives one pause for reflection on the state of macro-economics.

[3] M. H. Miller, *op. cit.*, p. 516, where he argues that incomes policy was a significant factor in the inflation in 1974-75 and also an important ingredient in the containment of inflation from the end of 1975 onwards.

ists in early 1974.[1] And this period provides an interesting test case for monetary predictions.

From the end of 1973 monetary growth declined sharply from an annual rate of approximately 25 per cent for the period September 1971-September 1973 to about 10 per cent. This *fall* in the growth rate of the money stock was associated, however, with highly *expansionary* public spending and budgets.[2] Here, then, was an acid test – monetarists predicted a sharp slump, whereas Keynesians would look to expansion. The outcome was a virtually unequivocal win for monetarism. Indeed the slump of 1974-76 was sharp and prolonged. The monetarist prediction that the inflation rate of prices would begin to moderate some 2 years after the end of 1973 was also borne out as the inflation rate declined to 13 per cent (year to July 1976).[3] The consequences of the prolonged monetary squeeze which began at the end of 1973 have not yet run their course, although even at this stage the provisional conclusions are clear, and it seems impossible to deny that monetary contraction played a major role in causing the slump and the arrest of inflation.

VIII

EXPANSIONISM AND THE ROLE OF MONEY

YET THE role of money in today's thinking on economic policy remains curious. Some economists regard the money supply as potentially dangerous if there are sharp and sustained changes in its rate of growth. Others, and a very influential group, such as Lord Kaldor, regard a constant growth rate of money as doing no great harm – after all, if money matters only for 'orderly financial markets' and does not affect anything that really matters (such as real growth and inflation), then the monetarists are

---

[1] For example, David Laidler's evidence to the Expenditure Committee of the House of Commons, *Ninth Report*, Session 1974-75, HC-328, HMSO, 1974.

[2] The Public Sector Borrowing Requirements (PSBRs) were: 1972-73 £1,024 million; 1973-74 £4,479 million; 1974-75 £7,623 million.

[3] The path of price inflation was much influenced by the third effect of monetary stringency – the gradual contraction of the deficit on current account of the balance of payments. Britain had to cease exporting inflation (as in 1973-74), and prices rose to reflect the smaller supply of goods on domestic markets.

welcome to their little rules provided they do not interfere with the running of the real economy.[1]

The essence is that, although monetary control is accepted as of some importance, there is a broad consensus that the government still must regulate the economy by means of varying public spending and tax rates. As evidence, witness the widespread calls for a stimulation of activity – for Germany and Japan to 'expand their economies' – and for Britain to reduce her unemployment and launch the economy once more onto a growth path. There has been little loss of faith in the ability of economists to plan and to manage the economy and 'to get the economy moving'. True, no-one pretends that government should 'fine-tune' but that does not mean that the government should not strike the right note. Although there has been a welcome admission that economic management is not, even approximately (!), an exact science, there has been little or no erosion of the belief that governments can much improve growth and employment by an active policy of stimulation. Active governments beget growth.

Money control a limited check to 'spending sprees'

But, you may object, controlling the money growth will surely prevent any excesses. Alas, I believe it will help avoid only some of the most wild swings (such as the Heath-Barber expansion).

Britain can still go on a spending spree, financed by the import of foreign capital and by manipulating the exchange rate (as in 1974), with only a modest increase in the money supply. And the adoption of monetary rules such as DCE (domestic credit expansion)[2] that include foreign borrowing seems to me to generate more trouble than enough.[3] Ponder the present tempta-

---

[1] There is a group of economists who may or may not regard monetarism as bizarre, but who argue that foreigners – and particularly conservative Swiss bankers – accept the principles of monetarism, and so one must put on a show for them or suffer currency crises. There is, finally, a fringe of economists, such as Lord Balogh, who regard monetarism as absurd. But they regard all the laws of demand and supply as readily repealed for political purposes.

[2] [Defined simply as the change in the money supply (M_3) plus the deficit on the balance of payments. – ED.]

[3] I argued that the DCE rule would be massively destabilising in the Second (1970) and Third (1971) Editions of *Money in Boom and Slump* (Hobart Paper 44, IEA, 1969). Five years later, there was an interesting illustration of the mordancy of a constant DCE rule. A normal DCE rule, if applied in 1974, would have called for a massive reduction in the money supply – and a considerable exacerbation of the slump.

[28]

tion when there is a substantial surplus on the overseas accounts and the domestic economy is slack. The seasonal call for a massive expansionary budget is to be heard in the land.

These calls for expansion have also cleverly employed the tools of monetarism to advance their case. One interesting example is the 'full-employment' budget. This calculates what the public sector's financial deficit would be if there were 'full employment'. It was designed to remove that part of the public sector deficit which was due to the fact that employment was lower than 'normal'; and 'normal' for this purpose was considered to be an arbitrary definition of full employment. Now the Cambridge Economic Policy Group shows that the 'full-employment' budget is in massive surplus rather than the observed deficit – and hence establishes the case for balancing the full-employment budget by expanding public spending.[1] And the rationalisation of it all is still the 'something for nothing'.

IX

CONCLUSION

I CONCLUDE, then, that, since 1970 when these lectures first began, despite the accumulation of new evidence and experience, there has been virtually no fundamental change in the principles that have guided policy discussion in Britain. The most obvious and apparently far-reaching development – the adoption of monetary targets – is largely cosmetic and probably for foreign consumption only. When it proves more than a little inconvenient, as in 1970, it will be shed like an old coat and the mantle of the 'growth merchants' will be worn with pride once more.[2]

Persistence of false theories and policies

Finally, I must touch upon the conundrum which I mentioned at the outset of this lecture. Why do these false theories persist and

[1] Of course, one would get quite different prescriptions if the norm of full employment were regarded as, say, one million unemployed.

[2] For a number of reasons why, see Robin Pringle, *The Growth Merchants*, Centre for Policy Studies, London, 1977. As I wrote this lecture, in October 1977, the new wave of expansion began to surge. We shall have to wait and see whether it again overwhelms us, as in 1972-73, and what the consequences are.

why are they still accepted as the basis for the most far-reaching economic policies? As Robin Pringle has recently suggested,[1] the explanation may be simple inertia which has been institutionalised and fossilised. There has been a considerable investment of effort and money and persuasion in the management techniques of the British economy. There is a natural reluctance to write it off. But more than that. There is a strong incentive to argue that the guidance system has been a success. True, it failed in 1972-74, etc., but that period was extraordinary and probably unique. Such anomalies, it has been argued, can be incorporated easily into a theoretical approach that is fundamentally correct.[2]

The assessment of evidence in economics is rarely, if ever, without equivocation. We cannot appeal, as the physicist may, to stunning experimental evidence. Furthermore, the macro-economic models fitted by econometricians are constantly shifting and virtually impossible for anyone who has not worked on them to pin down and to understand their complexities. But there is a rationale in persisting with trying to discover the detailed manage-ment models, for there is always the possibility that research *may* eventually enable us to forecast accurately. Meanwhile, however, economists should not claim more than they can deliver.

Of course, it is difficult to admit ignorance. After all, we are a highly paid profession – surely we *should* know better than the layman where the economy is going and how to put it right. There is a powerful temptation to respond to this understandable demand.

Democratic process encourages expansionism

As Peter Jay showed in his sixth Wincott Lecture,[3] the democratic process itself is responsible for the demand for expansionism. And so the conventional models rationalise the expansionary role of government spending to eliminate unemployment and promote growth. Are economists then guilty of meretricious behaviour – rationalising what the customer wants, telling the political populist what he wants to hear? I do not know. Motives are im-possible to observe and difficult to guess. I do suspect that most

[1] *Ibid.*

[2] Mr David Worswick has argued this case in some of his recent publications, e.g. 'The End of Demand Management?', *Lloyd's Bank Review*, January 1977.

[3] *Op. cit.*

economists have virtuous motives: we really do want to do good. But we must beware of La Rochefoucauld's maxim 'Virtue would not go nearly so far if vainglory did not keep it company'.

But change is in the air. Just as the classical system of economic management was thought to have failed in 1929-33, so, I believe, the sustained view will be that the theory of the nicely-managed growth economy died in the 1970s.

The world is demanding some new economic messiah (such as some latter-day Keynes) who will persuade us all that he has the key to understanding much that is now shrouded in mystery. And where there is demand, supply will not be far behind. But, ultimately, it is the poor suffering public who will pay the penalties or reap the rewards; and they will call us to judgement.

The Wincott Memorial Lectures

Occasional Paper 33
The Counter-Revolution in Monetary Theory
First Wincott Memorial Lecture
MILTON FRIEDMAN
With a Foreword by Lord Robbins
1970   3rd Impression 1974   50p
'It was a brilliant exposition of the theory which he has done so much to develop. In practical terms his message was one whose relevance was immediately apparent to his audience. You can only contain inflation, the argument ran, if you control the money supply.'

Director

Occasional Paper 35
Wages and Prices in a Mixed Economy
Second Wincott Memorial Lecture
JAMES E. MEADE
With a Foreword by Sir Alec Cairncross
1971   50p
'Professor Meade rightly thinks that a voluntary incomes policy is neither practicable nor desirable . . . He is also opposed to anything airy-fairy; to anything which involves detailed intervention by government; and to complicated arbitrational value-judgement by Mr Aubrey Jones or anybody else at all.'

Economist

Occasional Paper 37
Government and High Technology
Third Wincott Memorial Lecture
JOHN JEWKES
1972   50p
'Professor Jewkes . . . raises many questions which demand further attention.'

City Press